Things a
Gentleman
Would Like to
Know
Concerning
Etiquette,
Health and
Exercise

DON'T RUN
INTO DEBT

DON'T RUN INTO DEBT

"Don't run into debt;"—never mind, never mind
If your clothes are faded and torn:
Mend them up, make them do; it is better by far
Than to have the heart weary and worn.

Who'll love you the more for the shape of your hat,
Or your ruff, or the tie of your shoe,
The cut of your vest, or your boots, or cravat,
If they know you're in debt for the new?

There's no comfort, I tell you, in walking the street
In fine clothes, if you know you're in debt,
And feel that, perchance, you some tradesman may meet,
Who will sneer—"They're not paid for yet."

Good friends, let me beg of you, don't run into debt;
If the chairs and the sofas are old,

They will fit your back better than any new set,
Unless they are paid for—with gold;

If the house is too small, draw the closer together,
Keep it warm with a hearty good-will;
A big one unpaid for, in all kinds of weather,
Will send to your warm heart a chill.

Don't run in debt—now, dear girls, take a hint,
If the fashions have changed since last season,
Old Nature is out in the very same tint,
And old Nature, we think, has some reason;

But just say to your friend, that you cannot afford
To spend time to keep up with the fashion;
That your purse is too light, and your honour too bright,
To be tarnished with such silly passion.

Men, don't run in debt—let your friends, if they can,
Have fine houses, and feathers, and flowers;
But, unless they are paid for, be more a man
Than to envy their sunshiny hours.

If you've the money to spare, I have nothing to say—
Spend your silver and gold as you please;
But mind you, the man who his bill has to pay
Is the man who is never at ease.

Kind husbands, don't run into debt any more;
'Twill fill your wives' cup full of sorrow
To know that a neighbour may call at your door,
With a claim you must settle tomorrow.

Oh! take my advice—it is good, it is true!

But, lest you may some of you doubt it,
I'll whisper a secret now, seeing 'tis you—
I have tried it and know all about it;

The chain of a debtor is heavy and cold,
Its links all corrosion and rust;
Gild it o'er as you will, it is never of gold,
Then spurn it aside with disgust.

HABITS
OF A MAN
OF BUSINESS

HABITS OF A MAN
OF BUSINESS

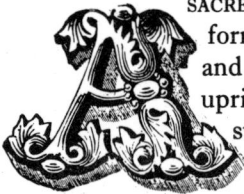

A SACRED regard to the principles of justice forms the basis of every transaction, and regulates the conduct of the upright man of business. The following statements afford a bird's eye view, as it were, of his habits, practice, and mode of procedure.

1. He is strict in keeping his engagements.

2. He does nothing carelessly or in a hurry.

3. He employs nobody to do what he can easily do himself.

4. He keeps everything in its proper place.

5. He leaves nothing undone that ought to be done, and which circumstances permit him to do.

6. He keeps his designs and business from the view of others.

7. He is prompt and decisive with his customers, and

does not over-trade his capital.

8. He prefers short credits to long ones; and cash to credit at all times, either in buying or selling; and small profits in credit cases with little risk, to the chance of better gains with more hazard.

9. He is clear and explicit in all his bargains.

10. He leaves nothing of consequence to memory which he can and ought to commit to writing.

11. He keeps copies of all his important letters which he sends away, and has every letter, invoice, &c., belonging to his business, titled, classed, and put away.

12. He never suffers his desk to be confused by many papers lying upon it.

13. He is always at the head of his business, well knowing that if he leaves it, it will leave him.

14. He holds it as a maxim that he whose credit is suspected is not one to be trusted.

15. He is constantly examining his books, and sees through all his affairs as far as care and attention will enable him.

16. He balances regularly at stated times, and then makes out and transmits all his accounts current to his customers, both at home and abroad.

17. He avoids as much as possible all sorts of accommodation in money matters, and lawsuits where there is the least hazard.

18. He is economical in his expenditure, always living within his income.

19. He keeps a memorandum-book in his pocket, in which he notes every particular relative to appointments, addresses, and petty cash matters.

20. He is cautious how he becomes security for any person; and is generous when urged by motives of humanity.

Let a man act strictly to these habits—ever remembering

that he hath no profits by his pains whom Providence
doth not prosper—and success will attend his efforts.

HEALTH IN
YOUTH

DEBERNY

HEALTH IN YOUTH

Late hours, irregular habits, and want of attention to diet, are common errors with most of the young, and these gradually, but at first imperceptibly, undermine the health, and lay the foundation for forms of disease in after life. It is a very difficult thing to make young persons comprehend this. They frequently sit up as late as twelve, one, or two o'clock, without experiencing any ill-effects; they go without a meal today, and tomorrow eat to repletion, with only temporary inconvenience. One night they will sleep three or four hours, and the next nine or ten; or one night, in their eagerness to get away into some agreeable company, they will take no food at all, and the next, perhaps, will eat a hearty supper, and go to bed upon it. These, with various other irregularities, are common to the majority of young men, and are, as just stated, the cause of much bad health in mature life. Indeed, nearly all the shattered constitutions with which too many are cursed, are the result of a disregard to the plainest precepts of health in early life.

RULES FOR THE PRESERVATION OF HEALTH.

Pure atmospheric air is composed of nitrogen, oxygen, and a very small proportion of carbonic acid gas. Air once breathed has lost the chief part of its oxygen, and acquired a proportionate increase of carbonic acid gas. Therefore, health requires that we breathe the same air once only.

The solid part of our bodies is continually wasting, and requires to be repaired by fresh substances. Therefore, food which is to repair the loss, should be taken with due regard to the exercise and waste of the body.

The fluid of our bodies is to the solid in proportion as nine to one. Therefore, a like proportion should prevail in the total amount of food taken.

Light exercises an important influence upon the growth and vigour of animals and plants. Therefore, our dwellings should freely admit the solar rays.

Decomposing animal and vegetable substance yield various noxious gases which enter the lungs and corrupt the blood. Therefore, all impurities should be kept away from our bodies, and every precaution be observed to secure a pure atmosphere.

Warmth is essential to all the bodily functions. There-fore, an equal bodily temperature should be maintained by exercise, by clothing, or by fire. Exercise warms, invigorates and purifies the body; clothing preserves the warmth the body generates; fire imparts warmth extern-ally. Therefore, to obtain and preserve warmth, exercise and clothing are preferable to fire. Fire consumes the Oxygen of the air, and produces noxious gases. Therefore, the air is less pure in the presence of candles, gas, or coal fire, than otherwise, and the deterioration should be repaired by increased ventilation.

The skin is a highly-organised membrane, full of minute pores, cells, blood vessels, and nerves; it imbibes moisture or throws it off, according to the state of the atmosphere and the temperature of the body. It also "breathes", as do the lungs (though less actively). All the internal organs sympathise with the skin. Therefore, it should be repeatedly cleansed.

Late hours and anxious pursuits exhaust the nervous system, and produce disease and premature death. Therefore, the hours of labour and study should be short.

Mental and bodily exercise are equally essential to the general health and happiness. Therefore, labour and study should succeed each other. Man will live most healthily upon simple solids and fluids, of which a sufficient but temperate quantity should be taken. Therefore, over indulgence in strong drinks, tobacco, snuff, opium, and all mere indulgences, should be avoided.

Sudden alterations of heat and cold are dangerous (especially to the young and the aged). Therefore, clothing, in quantity and quality, should be adapted to the alterations of night and day, and of the seasons; and drinking cold water when the body is hot, and hot tea and soups when cold, are productive of many evils.

Moderation in eating and drinking, short hours of labour and study, regularity in exercise, recreation, and rest, cleanliness, equanimity of temper and equality of temperature—these are the great essentials to that which surpasses all wealth, health of mind and body.

BATHING.

If to preserve health be to save medical expenses, without

DEBERNY

even reckoning upon time and comfort, there is not part of the household arrangement so important as cheap convenience for personal ablution. For this purpose baths upon a large and expensive scale are by no means necessary; but though temporary or tin baths may be extremely useful upon pressing occasions, it will be found to be finally as cheap, and much more readily convenient, to have a permanent bath constructed, which may be done in any dwelling-house of moderate size, without interfering with other general purposes. There is no necessity to notice the salubrious effects resulting from the bath, beyond the two points of its being so conducive to both health and cleanliness, in keeping up a free circulation of the blood, without any violent muscular exertion, thereby really affording a saving of strength, and producing its effects without any expense either to the body or to the purse.

WHOEVER FITS UP A BATH.

Whoever fits up a bath in a house already built must be guided by circumstances; but it will always be better to place it as near the kitchen fireplace as possible because from thence it may be heated, or at least have its temperature preserved, by means of hot air through tubes, or by steam prepared by the culinary fireplace without interfering with its ordinary uses.

A small boiler may be erected at very little expense in the bathroom, where circumstances do not permit these arrangements. Whenever a bath is wanted at a short warning, to boil the water necessary will always be the shortest mode; but where it is in general daily use, the heating the water by steam will be found the cheapest and most convenient method.

The late Mr. William Banting, author of a "Letter on Corpulence," gives the following excellent advice with a dietary for use in cases of obesity (corpulence):

1. **Medicine.**—None, save a morning cordial, as a corrective.

2. **Dietary.**

Breakfast.—Four or five ounces of beef, mutton, kidneys, broiled fish, bacon, or any kind of cold meat except pork, a large cup (or two) of tea without milk or sugar, a little biscuit or dry toast.

Dinner.—Five or six ounces of any fish except salmon, any meat except pork, any vegetables except potatoes; one ounce of dry toast; fruit out of a pudding; any kind of poultry or game, and two or three glasses of claret or sherry. Port, champagne, and beer forbidden.

Tea.—Two or three ounces of fruit; a rusk or two, and a cup or two of tea, without milk or sugar.

Supper.—Three or four ounces of meat or fish as at dinner, with a glass or two of claret.

Nightcap (if required).—A glass or two of grog—whisky, gin or brandy—without sugar, or a glass or two of sherry. Mr. Banting adds, "Dietary is the principal point in the treatment of corpulence (also in rheumatic diseases, and even in incipient paralysis). If properly regulated, it becomes in a certain sense a medicine. It purifies the blood, strengthens the muscles and viscera, and sweetens life if it does not prolong it."

The advantages to be derived from a regular mode of living, with a view to the preservation of health and life, are nowhere better exemplified than in the precepts and practice of Plutarch, whose rules for this purpose are excellent; and by observing them himself, he maintained his bodily strength and mental faculties unimpaired to a very advanced age. Galen is a still stronger proof of the advantages of a regular plan, by means of which he is said to have reached the great age of 140 years, without having ever experienced disease. His advice to the readers of his "Treatise on Health" is as follows:—"I beseech all persons who shall read this work not to degrade themselves to a level with the brutes, or the rabble, by gratifying their sloth, or by eating and drinking promiscuously whatever pleases their palates, or by indulging their appetites of every kind. But whether they understand physic or not, let them consult their reason, and observe what agrees, and what does not agree with them, that, like wise men, they may adhere to the use of such things as conduce to their health, and forbear everything which, by their own experience, they find to do them hurt; and let them be assured that, by a diligent observation and practise of this rule, they may enjoy a good share of health, and seldom stand in need of physic or physicians."

EXERCISE.

Exercise in the open air is of the first importance to the human frame, yet how many are in a manner deprived of it by their own want of management of their time! Gentlemen are for the most part destined to indoor occupations, and have but little time allotted them for taking the air, and that little time is generally sadly encroached upon by the ceremony of dressing to go out. It may appear a simple suggestion, but experience only will show how much time might be redeemed by habits of regularity: such as putting the gloves, shoes, &c., &c., or whatever is intended to be worn, in readiness, instead of having to search one drawer, then another, for possibly a glove or collar—wait for shoes being cleaned, &c.—and this when (probably) the outgoing persons have to return at a given time. Whereas, if all were in readiness, the preparations might be accomplished in a few minutes, the walk not being curtailed by unnecessary delays. Three principal points in the manner of taking exercise should be attended to:—

1. The kind of exercise.
2. The proper time for exercise.
3. The duration of it.

With respect to the kinds of exercise, the various species of it may be divided into active and passive. Among the first, which admit of being considerably diversified, may be enumerated walking, running, leaping, swimming, riding, fencing, different sorts of athletic games, &c. Among the latter, or passive kinds of exercise may be comprised riding in a carriage, sailing, friction, swinging, &c.

Active Exercises are more beneficial to youth, to the middle-aged, to the robust in general, and particularly to the corpulent and the plethoric.

Passive Kinds of Exercise, on the contrary, are better calculated for children; old, thin, and emaciated persons of a delicate and debilitated constitution; and particularly for the asthmatic and consumptive.

The time at which exercise is most proper depends on such a variety of concurrent circumstances, that it does not admit of being regulated by any general rules, and must therefore be collected from the observations made on the effects of air, food, drink, &c.

With respect to the duration of exercises, there are other particulars, relative to a greater or less degree of fatigue attending the different species, and utility of it in certain states of the mind and body, which must determine this consideration as well as the preceding.

That exercise is to be preferred which, with a view to

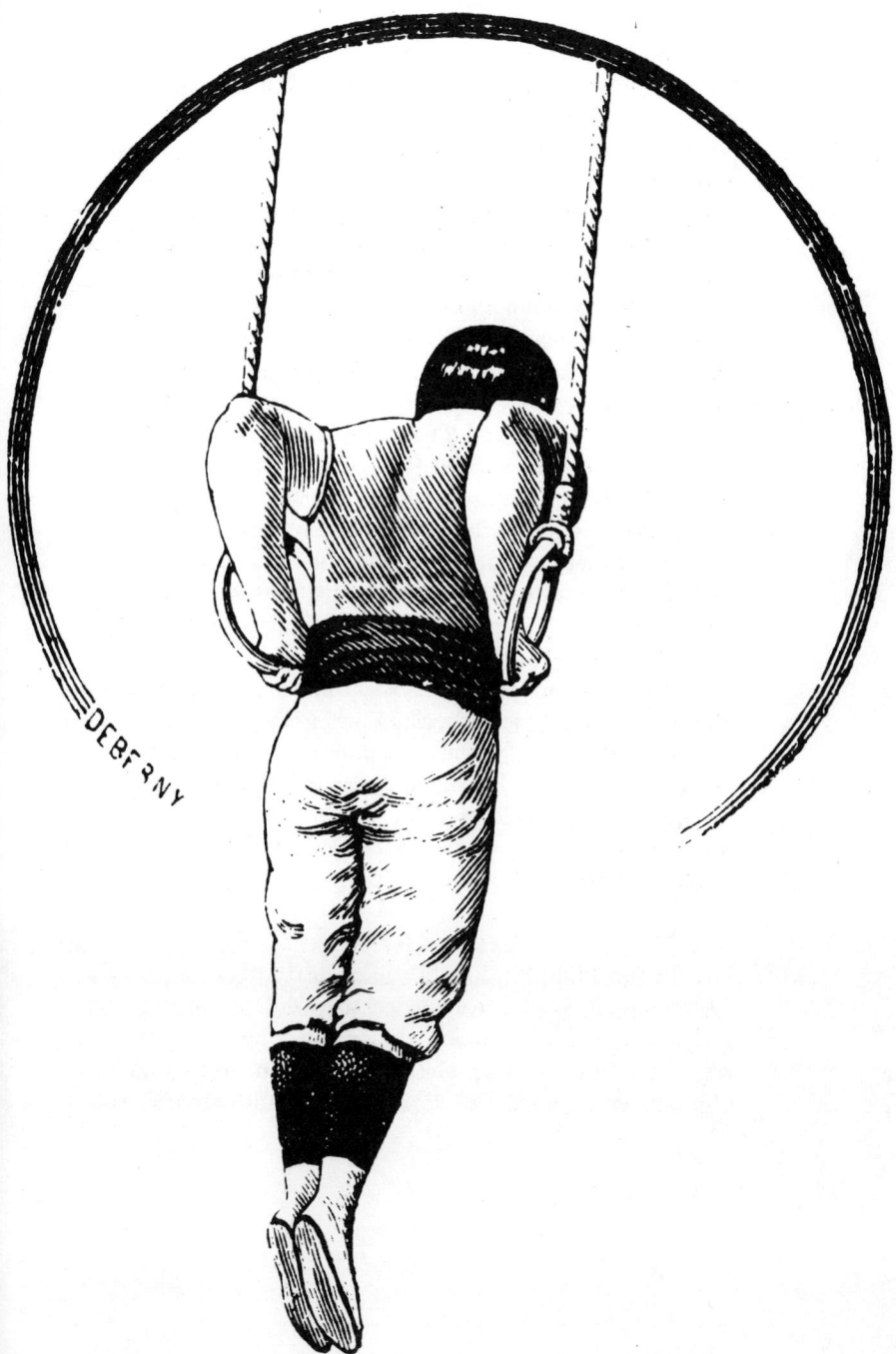

brace and strengthen the body, we are most accustomed to. Any unusual one may be attended with a contrary effect.

Exercise should be begun and finished gradually, never abruptly.

Exercise in the open air has many advantages over that used within doors. To continue exercise until a profuse perspiration or a great degree of weariness takes place, is far from being wholesome.

In the forenoon, when the stomach is not too much distended, muscular motion is both agreeable and healthful; it strengthens digestion, and heats the body less than with a full stomach; and a good appetite after it is a proof that it has not been carried to excess.

But at the same time it should be understood, that it is not advisable to take violent exercise immediately before a meal as digestion might thereby be retarded. Neither should we sit down to a substantial dinner or supper immediately on returning from a fatiguing walk, at the time when the blood is heated, and the body in a state of perspiration from previous exertion, as the worst consequences may arise, especially when the meal is commenced with cooling dishes, salad, or a glass of cold drink.

Exercise is always hurtful after meals, from its impeding digestion, by propelling those fluids too much towards the surface of the body which are designed for the solution of the food in the stomach.

EARLY RISING.

Dr. Wilson Philip, in his "Treatise on Indigestion," says: "Although it is of consequence to the debilitated to go early to bed, there are few things more hurtful to them remaining in it too long. Getting up an hour or two earlier often gives a degree of vigour which nothing else can

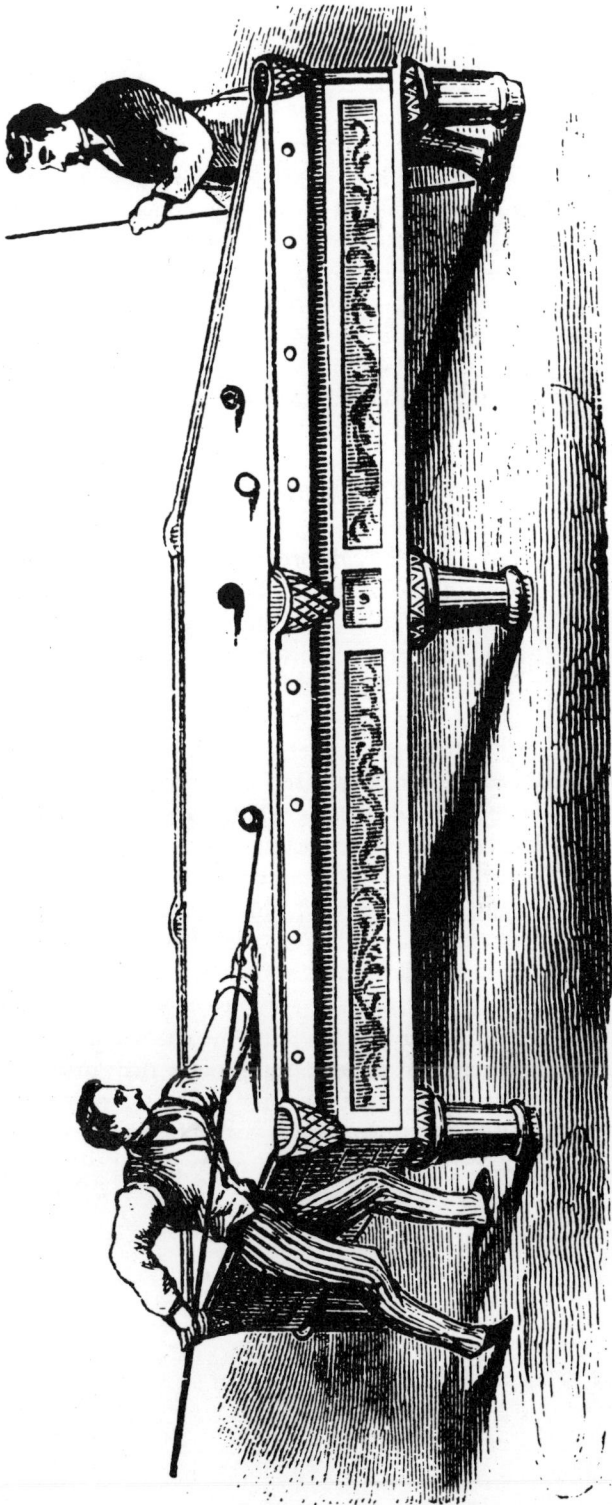

procure. For those who are not debilitated, and sleep well, the best rule is to get out of bed soon after waking in the morning. This at first may appear too early, for the debilitated require more sleep than the healthy; but rising early will gradually prolong the sleep on the succeeding night, till the quantity the patient enjoys is equal to his demand for it. Lying late is not only hurtful, by the relaxation it occasions, but also by occupying that part of the day at which exercise is most beneficial".

APPETITE.

Appetite is frequently lost through excessive use of stimulants, food taken too hot, sedentary occupation, costiveness, liver disorder, and want of change of air. The first endeavour should be to ascertain and remove the cause. Change of diet, and change of air will frequently be found more beneficial than medicines.

TEMPERANCE.

"If," observes a writer, "men lived uniformly in a healthy climate, were possessed of strong and vigorous frames, were descended from healthy parents, were educated in a hardy and active manner, were possessed of excellent natural dispositions, were placed in comfortable situations in life, were engaged only in healthy occupations, were happily connected in marriage, and kept their passions in due subjection, there would be little occasion for medical rules." All this is very excellent and desirable; but, unfortunately for mankind, unattainable.

Man must be something more than man to be able to connect the different links of this harmonious chain—to consolidate this *summum bonum* of earthly felicity into one uninterrupted whole; for, independent of all regularity or irregularity of diet, passions, and other sublunary circumstances, contingencies, and connections, relative or absolute, thousands are visited by diseases and precipitated into the grave, independent of accident, to whom no particular vice could attach, and with whom the appetite never overstepped the boundaries of temperance. Do we not hear almost daily of instances of men living near to and even upwards of a century? We cannot account for this either; because of such men we know but few who have lived otherwise than the world around them; and we have known many who have lived in habitual intemperance for forty or fifty years, without interruption and with little apparent inconvenience.

The assertion has been made by those who have attained a great age (Parr, and Henry Jenkins, for instance), that they adopted no particular arts for the preservation of their health; consequently, it might be inferred that the duration of life has no dependence on manners or customs, or the qualities of particular food. This, however, is an error of no common magnitude.

Peasants, labourers, and other hard-working people, more especially those whose occupations require them to be much in the open air, may be considered as following a regulated system of moderation; and hence the higher degree of health which prevails among them and their families. They also observe rules; and those which it is said were recommended by Old Parr are remarkable for good sense; namely, "Keep your head cool by temperance, your feet warm by exercise; rise early, and go soon to bed; and if you inclined to get fat, keep your eyes open and your mouth shut,"—in other words, sleep moderately, and be abstemious in diet; — excellent admonitions, more especially to these inclined to corpulency.

ELLIMAN'S
IN ADVANCE
ELLIMAN'S
ROYAL EMBROCATION
ELLIMAN SONS, & Co
MADE IN ENGLAND
AN
EXCELLENT
GOOD
THING.
Prepared only by
ELLIMAN SONS & Co.
SLOUGH.
ENGLAND.
ROYAL
FOR HORSES.
EMBROCATION.
UNIVERSAL
FOR ACHES & PAINS

HINTS ON
ETIQUETTE

DEBERNY

HINTS ON ETIQUETTE

HE WORD "etiquette" simply means "ticket", and is the "label" attached by an unwritten convention to the best observances in the social ike of well-bred people. The principles upon which it rests are clear and few in number. They may be enumerated as follows:—

1. Chivalry and delicate respect towards woman.
2. Repugnance towards allowing or taking a liberty.
3. Opposition to unwelcome obtrusion on the one hand, and to ungenial reception of friendly advances by equals in the social grade, on the other.
4. Hatred of fussiness and promotion of easy and natural demeanour.
5. Demand for reciprocity in favours and civilities conferred.
6. Recognition of the difference between civility and

servility, between kindness and condescension.

7. (And this runs through the whole code of English etiquette) Recognition of the fact that, at all events in this country, society is graduated.

From principles which never change, let us turn to the rules which guide most of the practical contacts of social life, but vary with the fleeting changes of fashion.

INTRODUCTIONS.

Be slow in giving "letters of introduction." By giving them you tax both the courtesy and hospitality of your friend. If the person to whom the introduction is addressed is in a superior station, it is only right to ask his permission before sending the letter. It sometimes happens that from early intimacy you yourself are willing to overlook many social short-comings in an old acquaintance, but that does not justify you in handing on to another one who has no right to expect indulgence from the friend of a friend. The letter of introduction should be closed and should be left with a card.

But apart from written introductions, the rule is good for general observance always to consult the wishes of both parties before the introduction is made. The following rules should be strictly observed:—

1. The lower in rank is always introduced ("presented" is a more courteous word) to the higher.

2. A gentleman is always "presented" to a lady never the reverse, and this without regard to difference of rank. (Of course at a ball, it would be futile to introduce a gentleman to a lady unless he was able and willing to be her partner in a dance.)

3. As regards introductions between gentlemen, it is difficult to lay down any rule beyond this that no one should undertake them unless he is sure that the introduc-

37

tion will be agreeable to both parties.

4. An unmarried lady is always "presented" to a married lady unless the unmarried is superior in rank. The ladies so introduced simply bow and make some passing remark. There is no need to shake hands. A lady's hand-shake is an act of grace, not of obligation, to a gentleman; he therefore waits after introduction for her offered hand.

5. The host shakes hands with all guests whether present by his own invitation, or brought by a personal friend.

6. At a dinner-party it is customary for the hostess to present the gentleman to the lady whom he is to "take down."

7. Gentlemen continuing at the table over "the walnuts and the wine" talk to each other without introduction.

8. In afternoon calls, the hostess uses her own judgement as to what introductions should be made, and such introductions do not necessarily involve more than bowing acquaintance afterwards. (Recent authorities say that the hostess should introduce all her guests to each other.)

9. In ball-rooms the real responsibility for introductions rests much more with chaperons than with stewards. The latter can only interpret according to their judgement the advisability of introductions. If an introduction is sought by a gentleman he is bound either to dance or at all events to show the usual civilities of the tea-room or supper-room to the lady to whom he sought to be introduced.

LEAVING CARDS.

1. Ladies govern all rules respecting the leaving of cards, which is an index to their choice of acquaintances, or the avowal that civility has been shown and is expected in return. A lady's card should always be plain in type, thin, unglazed, and not more than $3\frac{1}{2}$ inches in depth. The

address should be down in the left hand corner and the name in the centre. Ladies junior by marriage in a family, print their husband's christian name, but when they become the senior or sole survivors of the family, they change "Mrs. John Smith" into "Mrs. Smith." Young ladies print their names under their mother's name, if she is alive; if not under their father's upon a card shaped like a lady's card.

Gentlemen have certain rules of their own to observe in regard to making calls and leaving cards. A gentleman's card should be thin, unglazed, the inscription in plain English copper-plate with no flourishes after the manner of the Continent and America. Titles of persons of rank and of ecclesiastical dignitaries are never preceded by the definite article nor by adjectives such as "Most Noble," "Right Honourable," "Right Reverend," "Venerable;" nor do men with degrees or scientific or legal distinctions attach them to their names on their visiting cards. Thus correct use gives simply "Duke of Newcastle," "Bishop of London," "Archdeacon of Cleveland;" "Reverend Dr. Cooper." An "Honourable" drops the word on his card and is plain "Mr. Gordon." An officer in the navy adds R.N., or R.I.M. (Royal Indian Marine), after his name but no King's Counsel, Member of Parliament or Doctors of whatever faculty add K.C., M.P., LL.D., D.D. to their card-name. Baronets and Knights are simply "Sir Charles Forbes," "Sir William MacGregor," without Bart. or Kt. Officers in the army have the name of their club down in the left-hand corner and the name of their regiment in the right-hand corner.

1. In calling upon married people a gentleman leaves two cards, one for the mistress and the other for the master.

2. A gentleman should not turn down the corner of his card. His call is upon the host and hostess, and not upon

the young ladies of the house.

3. Calls are not made nor cards left by a gentleman upon new acquaintances, however pleasant they may have been to him at a dinner or ball in another person's house, without a clear intimation from the lady that a call at her house would be agreeable to her.

4. Bachelors call upon bachelors after receiving hospitality, unless they are upon such intimate footings as to dispense with ceremony.

PAYING CALLS.

Certain calls are obligatory, e.g., A formal call by you and a return-call by the person called upon is an indispensable preliminary to your inviting him or her to your house. Calls are different categories, principally these: calls of congratulation, calls of condolence, and calls of courtesy.

1. A call of congratulation is made upon a bride shortly after her new home. This is something more than a ceremonial civility and implies that you are prepared to continue herein, or admit her into the circle of your friends. You have, of course, already called upon her parents when the engagement was announced and after the marriage has taken place. Then again, on the birth of a child you call to "enquire after mother and child," leaving cards with your sympathetic enquiries.

2. Condolence is first expressed by a letter of sympathy bearing a narrow black rim in case of a death. You do not need to make your personal call until a card has come from the mourners "returning thanks for kind sympathy."

3. We now come to calls of courtesy or general calls. These are paid between the hours of 3 p.m. and 6 p.m., to allow the luncheon to be well over and preparation for dinner to be easily arranged. A few hints may here be servicable;

1. Visitors should never prolong their call beyond a quarter

of an hour or twenty minutes if they wish to avoid the charge of having inflicted "a visitation."

2. The hostess rises to receive her visitors and advances a few paces, but the other ladies present remain seated. (Gentlemen rise at each new arrival.) The hostess places each new-comer as near as possible to her own chair, and introduces them to those in their immediate neighbourhood to promote conversation. When they rise as about to leave she rings the bell, and the host, if he be present, hands the departing lady down stairs to her carriage, and bids her "good bye" (not "good morning") at her carriage door.

3. A gentleman brings his hat and stick (not his umbrella) into the drawing-room, and finds a convenient place to deposit them when he has occasion for the free use of his hands. (Often the floor is the most convenient.)

4. As regards refreshments nothing more at ordinary "At Homes" is required than tea, (which the hostess pours out herself), plain bread and butter, cakes, scones, and thinly cut sandwiches of pate de gras, &c., &c. On "big days" refreshments will be served in the dining-room, when claret, cup, coffee, &c., may be given.

VISITING.

1. In paying visits to a country house your task is now easier than of your in deciding the length of your visit. Your hostess generally specifies the time for which the invitation is intended, and this is no proof of scant hospitality. Necessarily the number of bedrooms is limited, and if a succession of visitors is expected your room will be required for the next visitor. Make your arrangements, therefore, rigidly with this in view. Consult Bradshaw beforehand, as to the time of your train for departure and do not appear to be hanging on in hopes of

43

an extended invitation. Young ladies and gentlemen, especially, are prone to jump at some such civil phrase as "don't you think you could spare us a few days longer?" which often is a *facon de parler* and nothing more. Of course there may be cases when there is no pressure for accommodation, and where, perhaps, the solitude of your host would make an intimate gentleman's-friend's extension of visit a real kindness. But this must be clear beyond dispute before you agree to go beyond the letter of your invitation. There is always a risk of outstaying your welcome. Sad indeed would it be if it happened to you as to the visitor of whom the old Scotch lady said to the cook in his hearing: "Jane, bile and extra egg for Mr. Brown's breakfast the morn, for he is gaun to traivel." Such a violent hint as this did he require before packing up to be off!

2. During your stay you will generally find the morning hours free. Breakfast and luncheon are "moveable feasts," and sometimes prolonged ones. It is, however, always well to ascertain casually from the hostess before saying "good night," whether she has any plans in which she wishes you to share next day. There may be a drive to a neighbouring ruin, or a pic-nic, &c., in which some or all the guests are wished to take part, and it would be unmannerly in you to absent yourself for some private pleasure. If there be no "plans" for the morning-hours, you can breakfast and take luncheon at any time during which the meals are running (9-10; 1.30-2.30) helping yourself from the sideboard and sitting down in any vacant place. If you are a fisherman or sketcher, you can always get sandwiches from the kitchen to obviate the necessity of returning for luncheon.

3. On no account, however, must you fail to appear in the drawing-room in proper attire at the hour prescribed

preparatory to going down to dinner. Some people are culpably lax in this elementary courtesy with the result of infuriating the cook, unnerving the hostess and angering all their hungry fellow-guests.

4. Try to make your host and hostess feel that you are enjoying yourself. "Nil admirari" is a wretched tone of mind to exhibit. Without violating truth in the slightest degree, you can always fix upon something in the house, grounds or neighbourhood which has given you pleasure. And to hear this moderately expressed gives pleasure to your entertainers.

5. Spare the servants unnecessary trouble by not ringing your bell upon every slight occasion, and reward them suitably upon your departure. But here comes a painful question: "What shall I give in the way of 'tips' or gratuities ('vails' was the old word) to the servants in my host's house, and to which of them?" Well, we are not all millionaires nor the guests of Dukes. It would be a real convenience if there could be, as in Holland, a well recognised tariff by which this melancholy business could be regulated for ordinary mortals. Of course, something depends upon the quality of your host and the length of your visit, but to judge by the countenance of servants, a short visit does not imply a material reduction in the gratuity expected. A week or a "week-end" is pretty much the same. Only general rules can be laid down.

1. From young girls little is expected.

2. From sportsmen gold is de rigeur; any default will be visited next season by the gamekeeper's relegation of you to an impossible place in the battue.

3. Fees to butlers range from five shillings to a sovereign. The servant who "valets" you always expects a special "tip." Half-a-crown is the usual gratuity given to a coachman, and even a young lady "remembers" the Jehu

who drives her to and from the station. She is generally exempt, however, from giving tips to other servants.

4. If no men servants are kept in the house, the parlour maid first and the housemaid second expect a gratuity. This may be five shillings in the first instance and half-a-crown in the second.

N.B.—Many men escape the difficulty of partition by giving a pound or two to the head servant and asking him to distribute it among the claimants. He is sure not to forget himself in dividing the spoil.

INVITATION TO DINNER.

1. The mode of reply to an invitation to dinner is governed by the mode of invitation. To a formal invitation the reply will take this form: "Mr. and Mrs. Burton accept with pleasure the kind invitation of Mr. and Mrs. Andrews to dinner on — of — at 8 p.m. (The day and hour are repeated in the acceptance to prevent mistake). Whatever the style of invitation the answer should be prompt, and the subsequent discovery of inability to be present (never except for the gravest reasons, e.g., family affliction, illness, or a royal "command") should be intimated at once. If one of an invited couple is obliged to withdraw, it should be left to the hostess to say whether she desires the presence of the other. As the hostess never asks anyone but a friend to fill up a blank ("the young man from Whiteley's" excepted), it is best for the stop-gap good-naturedly to accept, but the hostess ought verbally acknowledge the compliance as a favour.

2. The time of arrival should not be more than five, or at the most ten minutes after the hour named. Husband and wife do not now enter the drawing-room arm-in-arm, but the lady goes a little in front, and both make their way at once to shake hands with the hostess and then with the

host, without looking right or left to salute other friends. This imperative duty having been performed, the lady visitor takes a seat, but the gentleman remains standing and converses with anyone he knows. The only introductions made are those between the lady and gentleman who will go down to dinner together. The gentleman bows to his partner, but does not shake hands, and makes small talk until the announcement of dinner. When the move to the dining room is made, the gentlemen offer the ladies the right arm (because the lady will sit on their right side at table), the order of precedency being indicated by a nod from the hostess.

3. The following remarks refer to the usual observances at table:—

A. The guests unfold their serviettes and place them across the knee, not like foreigners who fix them inside their collar. The little nosegay inside the serviette makes a buttonhole. B. The menu card is glanced at, not deeply studied, for conversation, however light, must flow on uninterruptedly. The gentleman's first duty is to talk to the lady he "took down," but if during dinner she is briefly conversing with the gentleman on her right, he may talk without introduction to the lady on his left. C. Should the carving be done in the English fashion at the table, an opportunity is presented for one of the gentlemen who flank the hostess to offer his services. This should never be done by an inefficient carver, nor should a carver ever stand up to perform his task, however difficult. Bad carving tortures the heart of the smiling hostess and leaves the dish unsightly.[1] D. Three or four wine glasses stand at the right hand of each guest with a square of bread (intended to be broken, not cut) on the left. The small tumbler or the wide-cupped glass is for champagne, the ruby-coloured glass is for hock, the

smallest for sherry and the green one for claret. Sherry is offered with soup, champagne with the first entree, and then throughout the dinner. Hock or chablis is offered with fish, but there is no need to partake of all or any of these. Some people limit themselves to claret, whisky and soda, and others to plain water. Syphons of Apollinaris, soda water, lemonade, &c., stand on the side-board, and liqueurs (Chartreuse, brandy, Kummel, benedictine, &c.) are offered after ice-pudding.

4. The following hints are offered to the very few who may need them:—

A. Knives and forks are arranged in a fixed order. The table spoon is for soup, which must be eaten (need we say noiselessly ?) from the side near the point. The fish knife and fork are placed outside the others, ready for eating the fish which follows the soup. B. In helping yourself to dishes handed round, act quickly, and have regard to the wants of others, neither taking a microscopic portion nor a huge one. Never take two helpings of soup or fish even if asked, nor a large quantity of sauce. If you want a second supply of the joint, leave your knife and fork upon the plate when sending it to the carver. C. Aim at noiselessness both as regards eating, drinking, breathing, and every other possible source of disagreeable sound. Do not speak or drink with food in your mouth. Keep the moustache free from traces of soup, and use only the serviette in wiping the mouth. D. Eat curry with spoon and fork; sweet breads and vegetable entrees with fork alone, holding it in the right hand; oysters served on the shell with a fish knife and fork; fish rissoles and fish hors-d'oeuvres with a fish fork only; salads with knife and fork. E. Never use knife or spoon if a fork will do. With ice pudding or ices use a small spoon.

[1] For some hints on carving the reader may wish to refer to a companion volume *Things a Gentleman Would Like to Know Regarding the Social Graces*.

HUSBAND AND WIFE

DEBERNY

HUSBAND AND WIFE

H E UNDERTAKES no light task who ventures to give counsel in a relationship so ancient and so intimate as that of husband and wife. Many might think that the task was not only presumptuous but also superfluous, for who can hope to improve upon the counsel given in Holy Scripture, and summarised in the Marriage Service of the Book of Common Prayer and other manuals ? There is, however, a field which lies outside this technically religious territory that experience and genial common-sense, free from cynicism, may help to cultivate. Let us begin with a dictum which none will dispute: "Celibacy, however gloomy and painful it may sometimes be, is better than a bad marriage."

1. "In the selection of a wife, *tenderness* and *purity* are prime requisites, and no gifts of speculative intellect or practical ability can compensate their absence." ("Practical Morals," J. K. Ingram). The wife should be in fact:

"A creature not too bright or good
For human nature's daily food;
For transient sorrows, simple wiles,
Praise, blame, love, kisses, tears and smiles."

So sings Wordsworth in his exquisite "Portrait." And Byron, albeit not himself a model husband, is scarcely less successful in his "Bride of Abydos," in depicting the qualities expected in a good wife:

"To soothe thy sickness, watch thy health,
Partake but never waste thy wealth.
Or stand with smiles unmurmuring by,
And lighten half thy poverty."

2. But what about the choice of a husband? We cannot think of anything better as an answer to this question than the remarks of Mrs. Fitzpatrick in Fielding's "Tom Jones": "It requires a most penetrating eye to discover a fool through the disguises of gaiety and good breeding. . . . Among my acquaintances, the silliest fellows are the worst husbands; and I will venture to assert as a fact, that a man of sense rarely behaves very ill to a wife who deserves very well." *Sound sense*, then, is the indispensable quality which a young lady should require in the man who is to be her life-long companion. We place this first in the category, because even the highest moral rectitude and brilliant mental gifts, without the balancing power and prudential guidance of sound sense, will not secure her against the shipwreck of domestic happiness. Few sensitive people can watch, without disgust and loss of love, daily exhibitions of brainless, ludicrous, and stupid conduct on the

part of those whom they have sworn "to love, honour and obey."

3. There is one counsel that is applicable to both man and woman who are contemplating matrimony, and that is: Have regard to the approximate *equality* in birth and station, age and education, in the choice of a partner. Many centuries have rolled by since the great tragedian Æschylus put into the mouth of his chorus in *Prometheus Vinctus*, words which are just as true today as they were then: "He was indeed a wise man who first conceived in thought and then gave speech to his counsel, that to marry *suitably to oneself* is by far the wisest plan; and that one who is of low degree should neither seek after a partner lapped in luxury nor boasting of high-sounding pedigree." Gross inequality in any of the points named is sure to be visited with penalties more or less severe, but, in some form or other, sure to fail. Moderate disparity is of course less hazardous in consequences, e.g., an opulent merchant may find a hearty welcome in the family of straitened patricians, and a highly educated, untitled lady, well acquainted with the ways and manners of the "great world," may make an excellent wife for a nobleman, but nothing can compensate for a wide gap in years or education.

4. When we spoke just now of "approximate equality," we had in view only the particulars enumerated. Nothing can be farther from our meaning than to insist upon identity of tastes, predilections, favourite amusements, and the like. "Each sex has what the other has not; each completes the other, and is completed by the other; they are in nothing alike, and the happiness and perfection of both depends on each asking and receiving from the other what the other only can give." (Ruskin: "Sesame and Lilies.") It produces, for example, no jar in married life

for the wife of a scientist to be devoted to art, or for one consort to be passionately fond of sport while the other is equally enamoured of music or the drama. In fact, life is enriched by this non-antagonistic variety. Echoes are not needed for connubial bliss. Antithesis is often its charm.

5. Viewing marriage as a contract that involves the life-long obligation to cherish each other "in sickness and in health," it is of the highest practical importance to pay due regard to the question of health.

CONDITIONS OF MARRIED HAPPINESS.

1. No view of marriage is satisfactory that does not regard it as a tender and respectful friendship, "embellished," as a brilliant Frenchman adds, "by an incomparable mutual possession." We feel inclined to emphasise this view as of the greatest practical importance in perpetuating married happiness. The want of tenderness, either by the adoption of an over-bearing manner, which never reaches cruelty even in intention, or by what is still more characteristic of northern nations, the silence or sparse expression of love, even when it is felt, has a wearing effect upon its objects. A sentiment so tender as married love ought to be manifested. Much can be said against "gushing" and untimely demonstrations of marital affection, but undemonstrative conduct is not without its dangers. We have a terrible warning in the case of a famous teacher of his age, who learned too late, when his beloved one was taken away, how deeply he had failed in sufficiently expressing by word and act the feeling with which he regarded her.

2. Not less to be combated is the tendency for all the courtesies of the sweet-heart period to diminish, and sometimes to disappear, from married life. There should not be allowed to enter into the homestead any—even

good natured—disrespectfulness in language or manner towards any of its members. More depends upon the observance of this caution than many people realise. The only lady whom many a man habitually treats uncivilly, is his own wife; and the only gentleman for whom many a lady will take no pains to be pleasant and attractive, is her own husband.

3. Want of unity of aim is another prolific source of domestic failure. This has many sides, and enters into economics, child-training, the cultivation of good neighbourly relationships, the maintenance of a satisfactory footing with the relatives of both sides of the house, the relativity of work to relaxation, the quality and allotment of joint pleasures, and the formation of new friendships. Pitfalls in abundance attend every one of these illustrations of the want of oneness in aim. Unless there is mutual confidence as regards personal and household expenditure; unless each parent supports the other in the exaction of discipline among their offspring during the period of childhood, and a few years beyond it; unless each is complaisant towards neighbours and family connexions; unless they "see eye to eye" upon the ratio to be maintained between the serious and recreative portions of existence, and can co-operate in united tours, visits, expeditions and the like, and unless new alliances are the subject of mutual assent, troubles will grow in unlimited profusion "Union is strength" is an old adage; but in married life it is more: it is peace and comfort.

4. Hitherto we have spoken only of union in the practical concerns of wedded life, but no thoughtful person will undervalue the conviction "that any real and permanent union of human beings must rest on a sufficient harmony between them in respect of the three portions of our spiritual nature—feeling, intelligence, and what is

properly called character; and this harmony should be more complete in proportion as the union is to be intimate and profound" (Ingram). Profession of the same religious faith becomes, therefore, an important item in family concord.

To sum up in a nutshell all that we have said: The secret of domestic happiness lies in the exercise of mutual forbearance, gentleness and courteous demeanour, the desire to please and be pleased, the willingness to express pleasure when felt, the opportune demonstration of affection, and the determination to be one in aim and action in all that pertains to a common and co-operative life.

The Diet of all Lucky Dogs

Copyright.
Spratts Patent Ltd.

SPRATTS PATENT
DOG CAKES.

Pamphlet on **CANINE DISEASES GRATIS.**

SPRATTS PATENT LIMITED, BERMONDSEY, S.E.

USEFUL
INFORMATION

USEFUL INFORMATION

CLUBS.

Active, Service, 117, Piccadilly, W.
Albemarle (Ladies), 13, Albemarle Street, W.
Alexandra (Ladies), 12, Grosvenor Street, W.
Alpine, 23, Savile Row, W.
Army and Navy, 36, Pall Mall, S.W.
Arthur's, 69, St. James's Street, S.W.
Arts, 40, Dover Street, Piccadilly, W.
Athenaeum, 107, Pall Mall, S.W.
Authors', 3, Whitehall Court, S.W.
Bachelors' 8, Hamilton Place, W.
Badminton, 100, Piccadilly, W.
Bath, 34, Dover Street, Piccadilly, W.
Beefsteak, 9, Green St., Leicester Square.
Boodle's, 28, St. James's Street, S.W.
Brooks's, St. James's Street, S.W.
Burlington Fine Arts, 17, Savile Row, W.

Caledonian, 30, Charles Street, St. James's, S.W.
Capital and Counties, 42 & 43, Bow Lane, E.C.
Carlton, 94, Pall Mall, S.W.
Cavalry, 127, Piccadilly, W.
City Carlton, 24, St. Swithin's Lane, E.C.
City Liberal, Walbrook, E.C.
City of London, 19, Old Broad Street, E.C.
City of London Chess, 7, Grocers' Hall Court, Poultry, E.C.
City University, 53, Cornhill, E.C.
Cobden (no Club House), 28, Victoria Street, S.W.
Cocoa Tree, 64, St. James's St., S.W.
Colonial, 4, Whitehall Court, S.W.
Conservative, 74, St. James's Street, S.W.
Constitutional, Northumberland Avenue.
Crystal Palace, Crystal Palace, S.E.
Devonshire, 50, St. James's St., S.W.
East India United Service, 16, St. James's Square, S.W.
Eccentric, 21, Shaftesbury Avenue.
Eighty, 3, Hare Court, Temple, E.C.
Garrick, 15, Garrick Street, W.C.
Golfers', 2a, Whitehall Court, S.W.
Gresham, Gresham Place, E.C.
Grosvenor, 68a, Piccadilly, W.
Guards, 70, Pall Mall, S.W.
Isthmian, 105, Piccadilly, W.
Junior Athenaeum, 116, Piccadilly, W.
Junior Carlton, 30, Pall Mall, S.W.
Junior Conservative, 43, Albemarle Street, W.
Junior Constitutional, 101 to 104, Piccadilly, W.
Junior Naval and Military 96 & 97, Piccadilly, W.
Junior United Service, 11, Charles St., St. James's, S.W.
Kennel, 7, Grafton Street, New Bond Street, W.
Ladies' Army and Navy, 2, Burlington Gardens, W.

Ladies' Athenaeum, 31, Dover Street, Piccadilly, W.

London Polo Club, Crystal Palace, S.E.

Lyceum (Ladies'), 128, Piccadilly, W.

Marlborough, 52, Pall Mall, S.W.

National, 1, Whitehall Gardens, S.W.

National Liberal, Whitehall Place, S.W.

National Sporting, 43, King's Street, Covent Garden, W.C.

Naval and Military, 94, Piccadilly, W.

New, 4, Grafton Street, Piccadilly, W.

New County (Ladies'), 21, Hanover Square, W. and 84, Grosvenor Street, W.

New Oxford and Cambridge, 68, Pall Mall, S.W.

New University, 57, St. James's Street, S.W.

Oriental, 18, Hanover Square, W.

Orleans, 29, King Street, St. James's, S.W.

Oxford and Cambridge, 71, Pall Mall.

Pioneer (Ladies'), 5, Grafton Street, New Bond Street, W.

Portland, 9, St. James's Square, S.W.

Primrose, 4, Park Place, St. James's, S.W.

Raleigh, 16, Regent Street, S.W.

Reform, 104, Pall Mall, S.W.

Royal London Yacht, 2, Savile Row, W.

Royal Societies, 63, St. James's Street, S.W.

Royal Thames Yacht, 7, Albemarle Street, W.

St. James's, 106, Piccadilly, W.

St. Stephen's, 1, Bridge Street, Westminster, S.W.

Savage, 6, Adelphi Terrace, W.C.

Savile, 107, Piccadilly, W.

Thatched House, 86, St. James's Street, S.W.

Travellers', 106, Pall Mall, S.W.

Turf, 47, Clarges Street, Piccadilly, W.

United Service, 116, Pall Mall, S.W.

United University, 1, Suffolk Street, Pall Mall, S.W.

Wellington, 1, Grosvenor Place, S.W.
Westminster, 4, Whitehall Court, S.W.
Whitehall, 47, Parliament Street, S.W.
White's, 37, St. James's Street, S.W.
Windham, 13, St. James's Square, S.W.

Alhambra, Leicester Square, W.C.
Bedford, High St., Camden Town, N.W.
Camberwell, 23, Denmark Hill.
Cambridge, 136, Commercial Street, E.
Canterbury, 143, Westminster Bridge Road, S.E.
Chelsea Palace, King's Road, S.W.
Coliseum, St. Martin's Lane, W.C.
Collin's, 10, Islington Green, N.
Empire, Leicester Square, W.C.
Empress, Brixton, S.W.
Euston, 37, Euston Road, N.W.
Foresters', 93, Cambridge Road, N.E.
Gatti's, 214, Westminster Bridge Road, S.E.
Grand, Clapham Junction.
Granville, Broadway, Walham Green.
Hackney Empire, Mare St., Hackney.
Holborn Empire, 242, High Holborn, W.C.
Holloway Empire, Holloway Road, N.
London, Shoreditch, E.
London Hippodrome, Cranbourne Street, Leicester Square, W.C.
London Pavilion, Piccadilly Circus, W.
Lyceum, Wellington Street, Strand, W.C.
Metropolitan, 267, Edgware Road, W.
Middlesex, Drury Lane, W.C.
New Cross Empire, New Cross Road, S.E.
Oxford, 14, Oxford Street, W.
Palace, Shaftesbury Avenue, W.C.
Paragon, 95, Mile End Road, E.
Royal Standard, 126, Victoria Street, S.W.
Sadlers Wells, Rosebery Avenue, E.C.
Shepherd's Bush Empire, The Green, Shepherd's Bush, W.

South London, London Road, S.E.

Stratford Empire, Broadway, Stratford, E.

Surrey, 124, Blackfriar's Road, S.E.

Tivoli, Strand, W.C.

PLACES OF ENTERTAINMENT.

Agricultural Hall, Royal, Upper Street, Islington, N. Trade and other exhibitions and shows are held here, including the Military Tournament, Cattle Show, Dairy Show, and Horse Shows.

Albert Hall, Royal, South Kensington, S.W. Concerts and large meetings. The hall holds from 8,000 to 10,000 people and contains one of the largest organs in the world.

Alexandra Palace, Muswell Hill, N. Exhibitions and various Entertainments. The palace stands in delightful grounds.

Crystal Palace, Sydenham, S.E. Exhibitions, Concerts, etc. Beautiful grounds of 200 acres. First class Cricket and Football grounds and Athletic tracks. The final tie for the Association Football Cup is held here. Headquarters of the London County Cricket Club, which is managed by Dr. W. G. Grace.

Earls' Court, W. Summer Exhibitions, Large Theatre, The Great Wheel, Maxim's Air Ships, etc. Large grounds, which are illuminated nightly.

Madame Tussaud's, Marylebone, N.W. Celebrated Waxwork Exhibition.

Music Halls and Variety Theatres. *Under separate heading.*

Olympia, Addison Road, Kensington, W. Large Spectacular Exhibitions and Shows.

Queen's Hall, Langham Place, W. Concert Hall.

Royal Italian Circus, Hengler's, Argyle Street, Oxford Street, W. Circus.

Steinway Hall, Lower Seymour Street, W. Concert Hall.

St. George's Hall, Langham Place, W. Maskelyne's Home of Mystery.

Theatres. *Under separate heading.*

Zoological Gardens, Regent's Park, N.W. Extensive and interesting collection of animals, birds, reptiles, etc.

THEATRES.

Central London

Adelphi, 410, Strand, W.C.

Aldwych, Aldwych, Strand, W.C.

Apollo, Shaftesbury Avenue, W.

Avenue, Northumberland Avenue, W.C.

Comedy, Panton Street, S.W.

Court, Sloane Square, S.W.

Covent Garden, Bow Street, W.C.

Criterion, Piccadilly Circus, W.

Daly's, Leicester Square, W.

Drury Lane, Catherine Street, W.C.

Duke of York's, St. Martin's Lane, W.C.

Gaiety, 345, Strand, W.C.

Garrick, 2, Charing Cross Road, W.C.

Great Queen St., Great Queen St., W.C.

Haymarket, 7, Haymarket, S.W.

His Majesty's, Haymarket, S.W.

Imperial, Tothill Street, S.W.

Lyric, 29, Shaftesbury Avenue, W.

New, St. Martin's Lane, W.C.

Prince of Wales's, Coventry Street, W.

Princess's, 152, Oxford Street, W.

New Royalty (Theatre Francais), 73, Dean Street, Soho, W.

St. James's, King Street, S.W.
Savoy, Strand and Embankment.
Scala, Charlotte St., Fitzroy Square, W.
Shaftesbury, Shaftesbury Avenue, W.
Strand, 168, Strand, W.C.
Terry's, 105, Strand, W.C.
Vaudeville, 404, Strand, W.C.
Waldorf, Aldwych, East Strand, W.C.
Wyndham's, Charing Cross Road, W.C.

Suburban
Alexandra, Stoke Newington, N.
Borough, Stratford, E.
Brixton, Brixton Road, S.W.
Broadway, New Cross, S.E.
Camden, High St., Camden Town, N.W.
Coronet, High St., Notting Gate, W.
Crown, High Street, Peckham, S.E.
Dalston, Dalston Lane, N.E.
Duchess, Balham, S.W.
Elephant and Castle, New Kent Road, S.E.
Fulham, High Street, Fulham, S.W.
Grand, High Street, Croydon.
Grand, Islington, N.
Grand, Woolwich.
Kennington, Kennington Park Road, S.E.
King's, Hammersmith, W.
Marlborough, Holloway.
Metropole, Camberwell, S.E.
Pavilion, Mile End, E.
Richmond, The Green, Richmond.
Royal W., London, Church Street, Edgware Road.
Shakespeare, Clapham Junction, S.W.
Standard, High Street, Shoreditch, E.

Terriss, Rotherhithe.

Theatre Royal, Kilburn, N.W.

Theatre Royal, Stratford, E.

Great Central Railway, Marylebone Station, Marylebone Road, N.W.

Great Eastern Railway, Liverpool Street Station, Liverpool Street, E.C.

Great Northern Railway, King's Cross Station, Euston Road, N.W.

Great Western Railway, Paddington Station, Praed Street, W.

London, Brighton & South Coast Railway, London Bridge Station, South side of London Bridge, S.E., and Victoria Station, Buckingham Palace Road, S.W.

London & North Western Railway, Euston Station, Euston Square, N.W.

London & South Western Railway, Waterloo Station, South Side of Waterloo Bridge, S.E.

London, Tilbury & Southend Railway, Fenchurch Street Station, Fenchurch Street, E.C.

Midland Railway, St. Pancras Station, Euston Road, N.W.

North London Railway, Broad Street Station, Liverpool Street, S.E.

South Eastern & Chatham Railway, London Bridge Station, South Side of London Bridge, S.E.; Cannon Street Station, Cannon Street, E.C.; Charing Cross Station, Charing Cross, W.C.; Victoria Station, Vauxhall Bridge Road, S.W.; Holborn. Viaduct Station, Holborn Viaduct, E.C.; and St. Paul's Station, Queen Victoria Street, E.C.

A.WILLIAMS.DEL.   "W.KIRCHNER.SC

GAME SEASONS.

From a legal standpoint the word *Game* includes hares, pheasants, partridges, grouse, heath or moor game, black game and bustards.

No game can be killed or taken on a *Sunday* or *Christmas Day*.

LEGAL SEASONS FOR KILLING GAME.

Grouse or Moor Fowl.—For the whole of the United Kingdom, Aug. 12th to Dec. 10th.

Black Game or Heath Fowl.—Somerset, Devon and New Forest, Sept. 1st to Dec. 10th. All other parts of the United Kingdom, Aug. 20th to Dec. 10th.

Pheasant.—For the whole of the United Kingdom, Oct. 1st to Feb. 1st.

Partridge.—Great Britain. Sept. 1st to Feb. 1st. Ireland. Sept. 20th to Jan. 10th.

Bustard.—England and Wales. Sept. 1st to Mar. 1st. Scotland. No close time. Ireland. Sept. 1st to Jan 10th.

Hare.—Great Britain. No close time.* Ireland. Apr. 20th to Aug. 12th.

Male Deer.—Great Britain. No close time. Ireland. June 10th to Dec. 31st.

Fallow Male Deer.—Great Britain. No close time. Ireland. June 10th to Sept. 29th.

Quail.—Great Britain. As wild birds.

Landrail.—Ireland. Sept. 20th to Jan. 10th.

Ptarmigan.—England and Ireland. As wild birds. Scotland. Aug. 12th to Dec. 10th.

*It is not lawful to sell or expose for sale any hare or leveret in any part of Great Britain during the months of March, April, May, June or July. This does not apply to foreign hares.

Stag Hunting.—August 12th to October 12th.
Deer Hunting.—November 10th to March 3rd.
Fox Hunting.—November 1st to April 1st.
Hare Coursing.—July 1st to February 28th.
Otter Hunting.—April 15th to September 15th.

CLOSE TIME FOR FRESHWATER FISH.

Under this head "freshwater fish" includes all kinds of fish (other than pollan, trout and char), which live in fresh water, except those kinds which migrate to or from the open sea.

The close time for freshwater fish is from the 15th day of March to the 15th day of June, both inclusive, for England and Wales (excepting parts of Norfolk and Suffolk, where the close time is from March 1st to June 30th.

Any person who, during the close time, takes, sells, buys, or has in his possession for sale, any freshwater fish, is liable for the first offence to a fine of £2, and for subsequent offences to a fine of £5, with the following exceptions:

Owners of private fisheries where trout, char, or grayling are specially preserved may destroy within such fisheries any "freshwater fish" other than grayling.

Persons may fish in such fisheries with the leave of the owners.

Persons may take fish for bait or scientific purposes.

CLOSE TIME FOR TROUT AND CHAR.

In England and Wales, the general close time for Trout and Char is from October 2nd to February 1st, but there are exceptions. Any private owner can of course, within the legal limit, restrict the fishing in his own water. In parts of Norfolk and Suffolk the close time, for nets only, is from September 10th to January 25th. In the Thames from September 11th to March 31st.

CLOSE TIME FOR SALMON.
England and Wales.

The general close time for Salmon in England and Wales is November 2nd to February 1st for rods and· September 1st to February 1st for netting. The following are the exceptions:

	Rods.	Nets.
Adur . . .	Oct. 1 to Feb. 2	Sep. 1 to Feb. 2
Avon & Stour		
(Hants) .	Oct. 2 to Feb. 1	July 31 to Feb. 1
Avon & Erme		
(Devon) .	Nov. 30 to May 1	Sep. 30 to May 1
„ **(in Erme)**	Nov. 30 to Apr. 4	Sep. 30 to Apr. 4
Axe . . .	Nov. 20 to Apr. 30	Sep. 20 to Apr. 30
Camel . . .	Dec. 1 to Apr. 30	Sep. 21 to Apr. 4
Clwyd & Elwy	Nov. 15 to May 15	Sep. 15 to May 15
Conway . .	Nov. 15 to Apr. 30	Sep. 15 to Apr. 30
Coquet . .	Nov. 1 to Jan. 31	Sep. 15 to Mar. 25
Cumberland		
West . .	Nov. 14 to Mar. 10	Sep 15 to Mar. 31
Dart . . .	Oct. 1 to Feb. 28	Aug. 17 to Feb. 28
Dee . . .	Nov. 2 to Mar. 31	Sep. 1 to Mar. 31
Derwent		
(Cumb.) .	Nov. 15 to Mar. 10	Sep. 15 to Mar. 10
Dovey . .	Nov. 1 to Apr. 30	Sep. 14 to Apr. 30
Eden (below		
Old Sands-		
Field) . .	Nov. 16 to Feb. 15	Sep. 10 to Feb. 10
Exe . . .	Oct. 20 to Mar. 1	Sep. 1 to Mar. 1

	Rods.	Nets.
Exe (above Woodbury Rd. Stn.)	Oct. 20 to Mar. 1	Sep. 1 to Apr. 15
Fowey (below Lostwithiel Bridge) .	Dec. 1 to April 30	Nov. 1 to Apr. 4
Kent . . .	Nov. 15 to Mar. 31	Sep. 15 to Mar. 31
Ribble . . .	Nov. 2 to Mar. 1	Sep. 1 to Mar. 1
Stour (Kent)	Nov. 2 to May 1	Sep. 1 to May 1
Taff & Ely .	Nov. 15 to Apr. 30	Aug. 31 to Apr. 30
Teign . .	Nov. 1 to Mar. 2	Sep. 1 to Mar. 2
Usk . . .	Nov. 2 to Mar. 1	Sep. 1 to Mar. 1
Wye . . .	Oct. 16 to Feb. 1	Aug. 16 to Feb. 1
„ (above Bigs Weir Bdge)	Oct. 16 to Feb. 1	Aug. 16 to May 1
Yorkshire . .	Nov. 16 to Feb. 28	—

Ireland.

The close time varies considerably in Ireland. The following gives the general times in different districts for rod fishing:

Ballina	Sep. 16 to Jan. 31
Ballycastle	Nov. 1 to Jan. 31
Bangor	Oct. 1 to Apr. 30
Bantry	Nov. 1 to Mar. 16.
Coleraine	Oct. 1 to Feb. 28
Connemara	Oct. 16 to Jan. 31
Cork	Oct. 13 to Jan. 31
Dublin	Nov. 1 to Jan. 31
Drogheda	Sep. 16 to Feb. 11
Dundalk	Oct. 1 to Jan. 31
Galway	Oct. 16 to Jan. 31
Kenmare	Nov. 1 to Mar. 31
Killarney	Nov. 1 to Mar. 31
Letterkenny	Nov. 2 to Jan. 31
Limerick	Nov. 1 to Jan. 31
Lismore	Oct. 1 to Jan. 31
Londonderry	Oct. 11 to Mar. 31
Skibbereen	Nov. 1 to Jan. 31
Sligo	Oct. 1 to Jan. 31
Waterford	Oct. 1 to Jan. 31
Waterville	Oct. 16 to Jan. 31
Wexford	Oct. 1 to Mar. 14

Scotland.

The general close time for Salmon in Scotland is November 1st to February 10th for rods and August 27th to February 10th for nets. The following are the exceptions:

	Rods.	Nets.
Annan & Stinchar	Nov. 16 to Feb. 24	Sep. 10 to Feb. 24
Beauly		
Dunbeath		
Lossie	Oct. 16 to Feb. 10	Aug. 27 to Feb. 10
Ness		
Spey		
Bervie		
Carradale		
Fleet		
Garnock		
Girvan		
Howmore		
Inner		
Iorsa		
Irvine		
Laggan	Nov. 1 to Feb. 24	Sep. 10 to Feb. 24
Luce		
Sorn		
Ugie		
Ythan		
All rivers in Harris		
Bembecula		
N. Uist		
Orkney		
Earn	Nov. 1 to Jan. 31	—
Forth	Oct. 16 to Jan. 14	—
Hope & Polla	Sep. 11 to Jan. 10	—

	Rods.	Nets.
Nith . . .	Nov. 15 to Feb. 24	Sep. 10 to Feb. 24
Tay . . .	Oct. 16 to Jan. 14	Aug. 21 to Feb. 4
Thurso . .	Sep. 15 to Jan. 10	—
Tweed . .	Dec. 1 to Jan. 31	—

Dew.—If the dew lies plentifully on the grass after a fair day, it is a sign of another fair day. If not, and there is now wind, rain must follow. A red evening portends fine weather; but if the redness spreads too far upwards from the horizon in the evening, and especially in the morning, it foretells wind or rain, or both.

Colour of sky.—When the sky, in rainy weather, is tinged with sea green, the rain will increase; if with deep blue, it will be showery.

Clouds.—Previous to much rain falling, the clouds grow bigger, and increase very fast, especially before thunder. When the clouds are formed like fleeces, but dense in the middle and bright towards the edges, with the sky bright they are signs of a frost, with hail, snow, or rain. If clouds form high in air, in thin white trains like locks of wool, they portend wind, and probably rain. When a general cloudiness covers the sky, and small black fragments of clouds fly underneath, they are a sure sign of rain, and probably will be lasting. Two currents of clouds always portend rain, and, in summer, thunder.

Heavenly bodies.—A haziness in the air, which dims the sun's light, and makes the orb appear whitish, or ill-defined—or at night, if the moon and stars grow dim, and a ring encircles the former, rain will follow. If the sun's rays appear like Moses' horns—if white at setting, or shorn of his rays, or if he goes down into a bank of clouds in the horizon, bad weather is to be expected. If the moon looks pale and dim, we expect rain; if red, wind; and if of her natural colour, with a clear sky, fair weather. If the moon is rainy throughout, it will clear at the change, and, perhaps, the rain return a few days after. If fair throughout, and rain at the change, the fair weather will probably return on the fourth or fifth day.

Weather precautions.—If the weather appears doubtful, always take the precaution of having an umbrella when you go out, as you thereby avoid the chance of getting wet—or encroaching under a friend's umbrella— or being under the necessity of borrowing one, which involves the trouble of returning it, and possibly puts the lender to inconvenience.

Leech Barometer.—Take an eight-ounce phial, and put in it three gills of water, and place in it a healthy leech, changing the water in summer once a week, and in winter once in a fortnight, and it will most accurately prognosticate the weather. If the weather is to be fine, the leech lies motionless at the bottom of the glass, and coiled together in a spiral form; if rain may be expected, it will creep up to the top of its lodgings, and remain there till the weather is settled; if we are to have wind, it will move through its habitation with amazing swiftness, and seldom goes to rest till it begins to blow hard; if a remarkable storm of thunder and rain is to succeed, it will lodge for some days before almost continually out of the water, and discover great uneasiness in violent throes and convulsive-like motions; in frost as in clear summer-like weather it lies constantly at the bottom; and in snow as in rainy weather it pitches its dwelling in the very mouth of the phial. The top should be covered over with a piece of muslin.

The Chemical Barometer.—Take a long narrow bottle, such as an old-fashioned Eau-de-Cologne bottle, and put into it two and an a half drachms of camphor, and eleven drachms of spirit of wine; when the camphor is dissolved, which it will readily do by slight agitation, add the following mixture:—Take water, nine drachms; nitrate of potash (saltpetre), thirty-eight grains; and muriate of ammonia (sal ammoniac), thirty-eight grains. Dissolve these salts in the water prior to mixing with the camphorated spirit; then shake the whole well together. Cork the bottle well, and wax the top, but afterwards make a very small aperture in the cork with a red-hot needle. The bottle may then be hung up, or placed in any stationary position. By observing the different appearances which the materials assume, as the weather changes, it becomes an excellent prognosticator of a coming storm or of fine weather.

Hints on the Barometer.—*Why does a Barometer indicate the Pressure of the Atmosphere ?*
Because it consists of a tube containing quicksilver, closed at one end and open at the other, so that the pressure of air upon the open end balances the weight of the column of mercury (quicksilver); and when the pressure of the air upon the open surface of the mercury increases or decreases, the mercury rises or falls in response thereto.

Why is a Barometer called also a "Weather Glass" ?
Because changes in the weather are generally preceded by alterations in the atmospheric pressure. But we cannot perceive those changes as they gradually occur; the alteration in the height of the column of mercury, therefore, enables us to know that atmospheric changes are taking place, and by observation we are enabled to determine certain rules by which the state of the weather may be foretold with considerable probability.

Why does the hand of the weather dial change its position when the column of mercury rises or falls ?

Because a weight which floats upon the open surface of the mercury is attached to a string, having a nearly equal weight at the other extremity; the string is laid over a revolving pivot, to which the hand is fixed, and the friction of the string turns the hand as the mercury rises or falls.

Why does tapping the face of the Barometer sometimes cause the hand to move ?

Because the weight on the surface of the mercury frequently leans against the side of the tube, and does not move freely. And, also, the mercury clings to the sides of the tube by capillary attraction; therefore, tapping on the face of the barometer sets the weight free, and overcomes the attraction which impedes the rise or fall of the mercury.

Why does the fall of the Barometer denote the approach of rain ?

Because it shows that as the air cannot support the full weight of the column of mercury, the atmosphere must be thin with watery vapours.

Why does the rise of the Barometer denote the approach of fine weather ?

Because the external air, becoming dense, and free from highly elastic vapours presses with increased force upon the mercury upon which the weight floats; that weight, therefore, sinks in the short tube as the mercury rises in the long one, and in sinking, turns the hand to Change, Fair, &c.

When does the Barometer stand highest ?

When there is a duration of frost, or when north-easterly winds prevail.

Why does the Barometer stand highest at those times ?
Because the atmosphere is exceedingly dry and dense, and
fully balances the weight of the column of mercury.
When does the Barometer stand lowest ?
When a thaw follows a long frost, or when south-west
winds prevail.
Why does the Barometer stand lowest at these times ?
Because much moisture exists in the air, by which it is
rendered less dense and heavy.

WEIGHTS AND MEASURES.
LONG MEASURE.

12 lines	=	1 inch.	*in.*
12 inches	=	1 foot.	*ft.*
3 feet	=	1 yard.	*yd.*
5½ yards.................	=	1 pole, or rod.	*pl.*
40 poles (220 yards)........	=	1 furlong.	*fur.*
8 furlongs (1,760 yards)	=	1 mile.	*ml.*
3 miles (5,280 yards)	=	1 league.	

---

3 barleycorns	=	1 inch.
2¼ inches	=	1 nail.
3 inches	=	1 palm.
4 inches	=	1 hand (used in measuring the height of a horse).
9 inches	=	1 span.
18 inches	=	1 cubit.
2½ feet	=	1 pace (military).
5 feet	=	1 pace (geometrical).

GENERAL.

12 articles	=	1 dozen.
12 dozen	=	1 gross.
12 gross	=	1 great gross.
20 articles	=	1 score.
5 score	=	1 hundred.
6 score	=	1 great hundred.

NAUTICAL MEASURE.

Cables' lengths are nearly always used in Marine chart reckonings.

6 feet	=	1 fathom.
120 fathoms	=	1 cable's length.
2027·3 yards	=	1 knot or nautical mile.
3 knots	=	1 nautical league.

69·121 statute miles   =   1 degree.
   60 knots ......   =   1 degree.
  360 degrees ....   =   the circumference of the earth.

COTTON YARN MEASURE.

120 yards.........................   =   1 skein.
  7 skeins ....   =   1 hank.
 18 hanks ....   =   1 spindle.

COAL WEIGHT.

"All coal shall be sold by weight only, except where by the written consent of the purchaser it is sold by boat load or by waggons or tubs delivered from the colliery into the works of the purchaser.

Where any quantity of coal exceeding two hundredweight is delivered by means of any vehicle to a purchaser, the seller of the coal shall deliver, or cause to be delivered, or to be sent by post or otherwise, to the purchaser or to his servant, before any part of the coal is unloaded, a ticket or note according to the form following:—

Mr. A. B. (*here insert the name of the buyer*).
Take notice that you are to receive herewith......tons ......cwt......lbs. of coal.

(*When sold in sacks, add*)
in......sacks, each containing......cwt.

(*When sold in bulk, add*)

	tons	cwt.	lbs.
Weight of coal and vehicle.			
Tare weight of vehicle.			

Net weight of coal herewith
   delivered to purchaser....

         C. D. (*here insert the name of the seller*).
 E. F. (*here insert the name of the person in charge of the vehicle.*")—[*Weights and Measures Act,* 1889.]

COAL WEIGHT.

14 pounds	=	1 stone.
28 pounds	=	1 quarter.
112 pounds	=	1 hundredweight.
20 hundredweight	=	1 ton.
1 sack	=	1 hundredweight.
1 large sack	=	2 hundredweight.
21 tons 4 cwt.	=	1 barge or keel.
20 keels (424 tons)	=	1 shipload.
7 tons	=	1 room.

Truckloads vary, but contain from 7 to 10 tons.

BUTTER AND CHEESE WEIGHT.

8 pounds	=	1 clove.
56 pounds	=	1 firkin.
84 pounds	=	1 tub.
112 pounds	=	1 Dutch cask.
224 pounds	=	1 barrel.
256 pounds	=	1 Suffolk wey.
336 pounds	=	1 Essex wey.

FISH WEIGHT AND MEASURE.

1 barrel (of anchovies)	=	30 pounds.
1 quintal	=	112 pounds.
1 box (of salmon)	=	120 to 130 pounds.
4 fish	=	1 warp.
33 warps (132 fish)	=	1 long hundred.
10 long hundred (1,320 fish)	=	1 thousand.
10 thousand (13,200 fish)	=	1 last
500 herrings	=	1 cade.
1,000 sprats	=	1 cade.
600 herrings	=	1 mease.
615 herrings	=	1 maze.

FLOUR WEIGHT.

14 pounds	=	1 peck or stone.
56 pounds	=	1 bushel.
40 pounds	=	1 boll.
96 pounds	=	1 barrel.
80 pounds	=	1 sack.

WORSTED YARN MEASURE.

80 yards	=	1 skein.
7 skeins	=	1 hank.
144 hanks	=	1 gross.

LINEN YARN MEASURE.

300 yards	=	1 cut.
12 cuts	=	1 hank.
16 hanks	=	1 bundle.

CLOTH MEASURE.

This measure is used in measuring cloths, linens, silks, ribbons, muslins, tapes, tapestries, &c. Scotch and Irish linens, &c., are measured by the yard; Dutch linens bought by the Flemish ell and sold by the English ell; and tapestry is sold by the Flemish ell.

$2\frac{1}{4}$ inches	=	1 nail.
4 nails	=	1 quarter (of a yard).
3 quarters	=	1 Flemish ell.
4 quarters	=	1 yard.
5 quarters	=	1 English ell.
6 quarters	=	1 French ell.

TIMBER MEASURE.

1 load of unhewn timber	=	40 cubic feet.
1 load of squared timber	=	50 cubic feet.
1 ton of shipping	=	42 cubic feet.
1 stack	=	108 cubic feet.
1 cord	=	128 cubic feet.
1 Christiania standard ..	=	103⅛ cubic feet (120 boards, 11 feet long, 1¼″ × 9″).
1 Petersburg standard ..	=	165 cubic feet (120 deals, 6 feet long, 3″ × 11″).
1 London standard ⎱ 1 Dublin standard ⎰ ...	=	120 cubic feet (120 deals, 12 feet long, 3″ × 9″).
1 Quebec standard	=	275 cubic feet (120 deals, 10 feet long, 3″ × 11″).
*1 square.............	=	100 square feet (superficial).

*Boards sold by the square can be any thickness, thus:—200 boards 6 ft. long by 12 ins. wide measure 12 squares whatever their thickness. If 1 inch thick, for instance, it would be 12 squares of ½ inch stuff; if ¾ inch thick, 12 squares of ¾ inch stuff and so on.

BREAD WEIGHT.

		lbs.	ozs.	drs.
A peck loaf	=	17	6	2
A half-peck loaf	=	8	11	1
*A quartern loaf...............	=	4	5	8½
A quartern (or quarter-peck) of flour.....................	=	3	8	0

*Bread is now usually sold in 4 lb. and 2 lb. loaves, which must be weighed in the presence of the purchaser (fancy bread excepted).
Bakers are forbidden by Statute to sell bread by the peck or quartern.

56 pounds .... = 1 truss of old hay.
60 pounds .... = 1 truss of new hay.
36 truss .... = 1 load.
 1 square yard .... = 6 stone of new hay.
 1 square yard .... = 8 stone of oldish hay.
 1 square yard .... = 9 stone of old hay.

STRAW WEIGHT.

36 pounds .... = 1 truss.
11 cwt. 64 lbs. .... = 1 load.
36 truss .... = 1 load.

MISCELLANEOUS WEIGHTS.

Almonds ....basket ....1¼ to 1½ cwt.
    „   ....seron ....1¼ to 2 cwt.
    „   ....box (Jordan) ....25 lbs.
Arsenic ....cask ....4 cwt.
Ashes ....cask (American) ....3½ to 5 cwt.
    „   ....cask (Russian) ....10 cwt.
Beef ....tierce of 38 pieces (Irish) ....304 lbs.
Bristles..........cask ....10 cwt.
Bullion..........bar ....15 to 30 lbs.
Camphor ....box ....1 cwt.
Candles ....barrel ....120 lbs.
Cassia...........chest......................60 lbs.
Cinnamon ....bale ....92½ lbs.
Clover seed .....sack ....2 to 3½ cwt.
    „   seed ......cask ....7 to 9 cwt.
Cloves ....matt ....80 lbs.
    „   ....chest....................200 lbs.
Cochineal ....seron ....140 lbs.
    „   ....bag ....200 lbs.
    „   ....70,000 insects to 1 lb.

Cocoa . . . . bag . . . . 1 cwt.

  ,, ... cask . . . . 1¼ cwt.

Coffee . . . . barrel or robin . . . . 1 to 1½ cwt.

  ,, ... bag . . . . 1¼ to 1½ cwt.

  ,, ... tierce . . . . 5 to 7 cwt.

  ,, ... bale (Mocha) . . . . 2 to 2½ cwt.

Copperas . . . . hhd. . . . . 16 to 20 cwt.

Currants . . . . caroteel . . . . 5 to 9 cwt.

  ,, ... butt . . . . 15 to 20 cwt.

Feathers . . . . bale . . . . 1 cwt.

Figs . . . . drum (Turkey) . . . . 24 lbs.

  ,, ... frail (Faro) . . . . 32 lbs.

  ,, ... frail (Malaga) . . . . 56 lbs.

Flax . . . . matt. (Dutch) . . . . 126 lbs.

  ,, ... bale (Flemish) . . . . 2 cwt.

  ,, ... bale (Russian) . . . . 5 to 6 cwt.

Galls . . . . sack . . . . 3½ cwt.

Ginger . . . . bag (Jamaica) . . . . 1 cwt.

  ,, ... bag (E. Indies) . . . . 1 cwt.

  ,, ... bag (Barbados) . . . . 1¼ cwt.

Glass . . . . stone . . . . 5 lbs.

  ,, ... seam . . . . 24 stone.

Gum . . . . chest (Turkey) . . . . 4 cwt.

  ,, Arabic . . . . . chest (E. Indies) . . . . 6 cwt.

Gunpowder . . . . . barrel . . . . 100 lbs.

  ,, ... last (24 barrels) . . . . 2,400 lbs.

Hemp . . . . stone . . . . 32 lbs.

Hops . . . . pocket . . . . 1 to 2 cwt.

  ,, ... bag . . . . 2½ cwt.

Honey . . . . gallon . . . . 12 lbs.

Indigo . . . . seron . . . . 250 lbs.

Lead . . . . fodder or fother . . . . 19½ cwt.

Liquorice juice . . . case . . . . 1½ cwt.

MISCELLANEOUS WEIGHTS.

Mace ....case ....1½ cwt.

Madder ....cask ....15 to 23 cwt.

Magnesia ....chest ....1 cwt.

Meat ....stone ....8 lbs.

Molasses ....punch ....10 to 12 cwt.

Mustard.........cask (small).............9 to 18 lbs.

,, ...cask (large) ....18 to 36 lbs.

Nutmegs ....cask ....200 lbs.

Nuts............bag (Barcelona) ....126 lbs.

,, ...bag (Messina) ....1½ to 1¾ cwt.

Opium ....chest (Turkey) ....136 lbs.

,, ...chest (E. Indies)...........149⅓ lbs.

Pepper ....bag (free trade) ....¼, ½, or 1 cwt.

,, ...bag (white) ....168 lbs.

,, ...bag (black) ....316 lbs.

Pimento ....bag ....1 cwt.

Plums...........carton......................9 lbs.

,, ...¼ box ....20 lbs.

Pork ....firkin (Irish) ....100 lbs.

,, ...tierce ....320 lbs.

Potash ....barrel ....200 lbs.

Potatoes.........cwt. ....120 lbs.

Prunes ....barrel ....1 to 3 cwt.

,, ...puncheon ....10 cwt.

Quicksilver ......bottle ....84 lbs.

Rags ....bale (Hamburg).............2¼ cwt.

,, ...bale (Mediterranean) ....4¼ to 5 cwt.

Resin ....barrel ....about 2 cwt.

Raisins ....drum (Valencia) ....24 lbs.

,, ...box ,, ... 30 to 40 lbs.

,, ...cask (Malaga) ....1 cwt.

,, ...box ,, ...22 lbs.

,, ...cask (Turkey) ....2½ cwt.

Rice ....bag (E. Indies) ....1½ cwt.
  ,, ...cask (America)...............6 cwt.
Sago............bag ....1 cwt.
Salmon ....box.................120 to 130 lbs.
Salt............bushel ....56 lbs.
Saltpetre ....bag ....1½ cwt.
  ,, ...barrel ....1 cwt.
Shellac..........chest ....1 to 3 cwt.
Soap...........firkin ....64 lbs.
  ,, ...barrel....................,256 lbs.
  ,, ...chest ....3¼ cwt.
Soda...........cask ....3 to 4 cwt.
Steel...........fagot....................120 lbs.
Sugar ....bag (E. Indies) ....1 to 1¾ cwt.
  ,, ...matt or bag (Mauritius)..1 to 1½ cwt.
  ,, ...tierce (W. Indies) ....7 to 9 cwt.
  ,, ...hhd. (W. Indies).......13 to 16 cwt.
Sugar Candy.....box........................70 lbs.
Tallow ....cask ....9 cwt..
Tapioca ....barrel ....1¼ cwt.
Tea.............chest (Congou).............80 lbs.
  ,, ... ,, (Hyson).........60 to 80 lbs.
  ,, ... ,, (ordinary) ....84 lbs.
Tiles...........load 1,000
Tobacco........hhd. ....12 to 18 cwt.
Turpentine .....barrel ....2 to 2½ cwt.
Vermilion ....bag.......................50 lbs.
Walnuts.........bag ....1 cwt.

DRY MEASURE.

4 gills .... = 1 pint.
2 pints .... = 1 quart.
2 quarts .... = 1 pottle.

DRY MEASURE.

2 pottles (4 quarts)	=	1 gallon.
2 gallons	=	1 peck.
4 pecks.................	=	1 bushel.
3 bushels	=	1 bag.
4 bushels	=	1 coomb.
5 bushels (or porter's load).	=	1 sack of flour.
8 bushels	=	1 quarter.
12 bags (36 bushels)	=	1 chaldron.
5 quarters (40 bushels)	=	1 wey or horse-load.
2 weys (10 quarters)	=	1 last.

ALE AND BEER MEASURE.

4 gills..........................	=	1 pint.
2 pints	=	1 quart.
4 quarts	=	1 gallon.
9 gallons	=	1 firkin.
2 firkins (18 gallons)	=	1 kilderkin.
2 kilderkins	=	1 barrel.
1½ barrels	=	1 hogshead.
2 hogsheads.....................	=	1 butt.
2 butts	=	1 tun.

WINE MEASURE.

4 gills........................	=	1 pint.
2 pints	=	1 quart.
4 quarts	=	1 gallon.
10 gallons	=	1 anker.
18 gallons	=	1 runlet.
31½ gallons	=	1 barrel.
42 gallons	=	1 tierce.
63 gallons	=	1 hogshead.
84 gallons	=	1 puncheon.
2 hogsheads....................	=	1 pipe or butt.
2 pipes	=	1 tun.

MISCELLANEOUS WINE AND SPIRIT MEASURES.

1 hogshead of Claret	=	46 gallons.
1 butt of Sherry	=	108 ,,
1 pipe of Port	=	115 ,,
1 pipe of Madeira	=	92 ,,
1 pipe of Teneriffe...........	=	100 ,,
1 pipe of Lisbon.............	=	115 ,,
1 butt of Malaga	=	105 ,,
1 aum of Hock, Rhine, or Moselle	=	30 ,,
1 pipe of Cape	=	92 ,,
1 hogshead of Tent	=	54 ,,
1 pipe of Marsala	=	93 ,,
1 puncheon of S. Whiskey	=	112 to 120 ,,
1 puncheon of Brandy........	=	100 to 110 ,,
1 hogshead of Brandy	=	45 to 55 ,,
Quarter-cask of Brandy.......	=	26 to 28 ,,
1 pipe of Cider	=	100 to 118 ,,
1 piece of Geneva	=	about 116 ,,
1 puncheon of Rum..........	=	90 to 100 ,,
1 hogshead of Rum	=	45 to 50 ,,
1 tun of Wine...............	=	240 ,,
1 pipe or butt	=	108 to 117 ,,